Like a B Movie

Jennifer Lagier

FUTURECYCLE PRESS
www.futurecycle.org

Library of Congress Control Number: 2017964648

Published by FutureCycle Press
Athens, Georgia, USA

ISBN 978-1-942371-45-8

For my mother
June J. Lewis

Contents

Mane Events

Scene of the Crime

Soberanes Fire

Malpractice

MANE EVENTS

Namesake

Jennifer Jones exuded piety,
visited a secret, sacred grotto,
innocently trysted with a higher power,
accepted prophetic messages
in the *Song of Bernadette.*
Despite decades of imposed Catholicism,
I never felt the gentle hand of God,
received angelic direction or was blessed
by preferment, descending grace.
Her role in *Love Is a Many Splendored Thing*
resulted in award nominations.
Illicit passion ended with a broken heart,
bliss aborted, aftermath bittersweet.
Like my namesake,
I burned through marriages,
squandered opportunities,
watched myself wither
as empty years passed.

Guinevere

"The Cornish form of this name, *Jennifer,* has become
popular in the English-speaking world."
                                        —Behindthename.com

I will never know if my father
was thinking of Arthurian legend
when he selected my name,
uncommon for 1949.

In grammar school, I was
the Italian-American Jennifer
immersed in a Scandinavian sea
of white bread Cindys, Susies and Anns.

Perhaps Guinevere's archetype
determined the unfaithful wife
I became, stumbling into adultery,
cuckolding multiple husbands.

After each devastating divorce,
a sisterhood of supportive women
helped me reboot, restart the cycle:
marriage, dying love, illicit passion, betrayal.

In My *What the Hell* Hat

I found it while browsing
in a funky Cambria boutique
while on a goddess getaway
for a week with two poet friends.

Tried it on, slanted wickedly
over one eye, loved the bad girl
looking back at me
from the fitting room mirror,
a perfect accessory for
my inner wild child, Camille.

I wore it that night as I sipped
multiple Rosarita Margaritas,
flirted outrageously with sexy guys
on the outdoor patio at
Moonstone Beach Bar & Grill.

Blamed naughty behavior
on the new *What the Hell* hat.
Felt my inner slut bloom.

Hard

At thirty, my husband
demanded I look and act
as if I was sixteen.
It was like forcing my foot
into a shoe three sizes too small:
cramming myself into a life
that no longer fit.

When we separated,
guilt made me report for duty
in response to his
once-a-week call.
He'd leave fifty dollars
on the night stand
next to his bed,
tell me I'd be
so much happier,
probably still married,
if I just didn't think.

After, I would
pump iron for hours,
run seven cross-country miles,
shower and scrub myself raw.
I pared away feminine softness,
built muscles of steel,
became invulnerable and invincible,
made myself hard.

Are You Experienced?

Ah, Jimi,
you had me
at the first erotic scream
of tortured riff.

Your fingers teased,
aroused the guitar,
left your audience
begging for mercy.

It was Pleasanton, '68,
me barefoot, stoned,
accepting every toke
I was handed.

Baby, you touched me
in places no one else
even knew existed,
left me shuddering.

If I wasn't experienced
before, I was after
embracing the ecstatic burn
of your hot purple haze.

Doppelganger

She tilts her head,
gazes through invisible frame,
candlestick visible above one shoulder,
just a hint of brass bed.

Her mouth gives nothing away.
Flat, parted hair, strong jaw,
long nose, narrow lips,
my doppelganger twin.

The fickle mirror reflects
my squinty, off-kilter eyes,
Modigliani neck, now wrinkled,
the same elongated face.

A forceful woman who
impatiently ploughs through obstacles,
pursues what moves her,
time on earth running out.

I determinedly wade into battle,
lead with my chin,
know death is coming,
won't give an inch.

Driver's Ed

Our high school class
took turns behind the wheel
of a column shift Chevy.
Read DMV handbooks,
then watched gory films
of horrific car wrecks.

Brake, clutch and gas pedals
required coordination
we had not yet mastered.
Kept us lurching across
an asphalt volleyball court
while our impatient instructor
stomped the floorboard,
grabbed the steering wheel,
barked orders.

Back home, in the orchard,
Dad ignored my protests,
insisted I move his truck
to make room for the tractor.
Grimaced but didn't say a word
when I side-swiped a peach tree,
amputated mirror, door and fender.

Autumn on Kauai

Pele's feisty roosters screech,
challenge the audacity of daybreak,
chase pompous Nene geese and timid doves.
Their crowing grates nerves, transforms to dream demons.

Rising sun sizzles against palms, pines, hibiscus.
Blushing rain clouds float above scarlet ti trees,
monster philodendrons, banana leaf jungle.
Swollen cumuli billow, suffused with tropical colors.

Blustery blue storms sweep ashore,
dump warm silver payload.
Battered plumerias revert to bare limbs,
autumn reflected in an absence of flowers.

Transported from arid California shores,
even the most austere succumb
to sensual saturation, perfumed head winds.
Brilliant, broken gardens let the soul blossom.

Hanalei Halloween

All Hallow's Eve on Kauai—women in cat's ears and whiskers,
a harem girl's outfit, pool boys dressed like the devil.

A Grateful Dead skeleton riffs beneath red bandana.
His stage—a carved pumpkin perched upon a faux cow skull.

Bat wings stretch, poised for flight within scarlet scarab.
Love beads wrap the base of a gravestone.

Candy corn, bedsheet ghosts, eight-legged plastic spiders.
I take refuge on the lanai, treat myself to a mai tai.

Cinderella's Support Group

Her cigarette shakes
during her turn
to describe how
happy-ever-after
went dramatically wrong.

She crumples Kleenex,
tells the traditional
rags-to-riches,
rescue-by-prince-
on-a-white-charger story.
Her stepsisters understand

the familiar betrayal motif,
smile wryly, nod when she
sobs about the poisoned apple,
the treacherous mirror.

She is over forty and
the magic is dead.
There are no cotillions left.
Youth's glass slipper has shattered;
the glittery ball gown no longer fits.

Exodus

School of Library Science, U.C. Berkeley, 1983-84

I packed my car,
drove away from you,
our cat, Galootie, the little house
we called The Early Bracero.
We wore sunglasses to hide
red eyes, flowing tears.

Took typewriter, journals,
a few clothes and photos.
Moved from small town
Central Valley to a bohemian
Berkeley basement apartment.

Left behind affection and laughter,
a perpetual gathering
of friends, writers, musicians
crowded around
our red kitchen table.

Surrounded myself with
fellow graduate students.
Wrote reams of poetry
between school assignments.
Ached during a loveless year
of scholarly exile.

Gastronomical Archive

My mother uses her black cookbook
with a broken spine
as a portable file
for historical treasure.
Here cioppino recipes
cohabitate with obituaries,
expired coupons and cards
for religious novenas.
"When I die," she says,
"I give my jewelry
to your sister.
But for you, I have
saved something precious."

Between Betty Crocker's
scorned printed pages,
my inheritance nestles,
yellowed cooking instructions
written with a leaky pen
on Sunday offering envelopes.
Secrets reside inside
this bulging cover
bound with rubber bands,
a hidden, tantalizing feast
of delectable pleasures.

Ho, Ho Humbug

Christmas expectations ruin Thanksgiving,
bring on bronchitis, paint me into a corner.

This year our diminished family will gather and grieve.
I mourn the missing and infirm, dread empty chairs.

Cooking, baking and decoration require days of attention.
Merchandise needs to be selected, purchased and wrapped.

It's my job to find, transport, then ornament seven feet
of needle-dropping Frasier Fir, our annual holiday tree.

The to-do list spirals out of control as I huddle under blankets,
cough and feverishly shiver, watch an icy rain spill.

With wheezing lungs, I drop Alka Seltzer tablets
into a glass, pray for relief as the healing hosts fizz.

If I Listened to Mom

If I had listened to my mother,
followed rules,
been a docile, obedient wife,
would I still be an independent,
educated, feminist,
free-spirited poet?

Looking back,
I discover a trashy B movie:
naïve virgin, married too young,
careless midlife adultery,
older reentry student,
homeless divorcee.

Immaturity and hard-headedness
disrupted predictable plotlines.
Chain-reaction disasters
forced me to learn survival skills,
reinvent self, keep starting over.

Without stumbling,
could I have still pushed boundaries,
discovered passion,
amassed a rich repertoire
of unique adventures?

Mane Events

A chubby toddler,
I possessed a few golden wisps.
When my 1950s pixie cut grew out,
Mom wove my thin hair
into tight, skinny braids.

By the early '60s, I wore
bleached, feathered highlights
over a ratted beehive
to accompany poodle skirts, fluffy slips.

During the Summer of Love,
I smoked dope, visited Haight-Ashbury
clad in Nehru jacket,
flat, ironed locks and leather headband,
paisley bell-bottomed pants.

The '70s brought women's lib
and a messy divorce.
I flaunted a blonde afro,
went braless beneath skimpy tank tops,
peg-legged tiny jeans.

During late '80s, early '90s,
I traded classic pageboy
for moussed punk spikes,
message tee shirts,
anti-war picket signs.

Now I wrestle faded cowlicks,
pay a professional to paint auburn streaks
through my anemic mane,
resurrect vanished youth.

Seduction

I've always hungered
for illicit thrills, the sweet forbidden,
preferred gorging on pastries
to sensible meals
of balanced proportions.

My wooden cooking spoon
whispers flirtatiously
to watering mouth, waiting hunger,
pursues tender apple slices,
grated cinnamon,
through shimmering butter.

Thick lemon custard
crooks a beckoning finger,
simmers with pungent zest,
wafts the scent
of promiscuous sugar.

Push-over dough
wants only to please you,
slithers beneath floured rolling pin,
spreads skinny pie crust.
The kitchen pulses
with erotic aromas.

I invite appetite
to pull up a chair,
settle in and feast
at my bounteous table.

Witch Hunt

You recall the tarnished rosaries
chanted weekly
to ward off bad blood,
remember the red pattern
tattooed by wire coat hangers
on a child's skin.

Frozen gray photos
from the Siberia of our attic
show the manicured party facade:
matching dresses, tiny hats,
patent leather shoes,
Sunday veils and white gloves.

You search for evidence among
nostalgia's boxed ruins,
find only the toxic soundtrack
which plays on endlessly, dropping
words like *incompetent, failure*
into dark seams.
Nightmares, fanged predators,
label every possible flaw.

You swallow whatever potion
will unwind the poisoned necklace of thorns,
undo a witch's curse,
remove the lethal apple pushed with love
down a little girl's throat.

Sleuth

"...as cool as Mata Hari and as sweet as Betty Crocker."
—Bobbie Ann Mason

Nancy Drew, you were exactly
what this naïve country girl needed.
Inquisitive and assertive,
you were a positive prototype
for generations of professional women.
Taught us to persevere,
dispassionately analyze,
constantly question.
Provided a model
of poise, independence.
I marveled at your cool skill
at unraveling mysteries,
identifying bad guys,
playing detective.
Mourned when publishers
decided to cut you down
to less-threatening size,
transformed your character
from dominant force
into decorative female.

Chain Store Hell

Thirty-year-old male supervisors
wore white shirts, black ties.
Possessing high school diplomas,
they earned lofty salaries,
passed themselves off
as the privileged elite.

We were "girls,"
chain store cashiers
paid minimum wage,
without benefits,
unwitting stars
of their erotic fantasies.

As we hurried from check stand
to break room, through
backroom warehouse gauntlet,
groping hands reached
over Kotex and toilet paper cartons
to detain and harass.

When their wives arrived
with crammed shopping carts,
we were cautioned not to act
too friendly or speak without adding
a respectful "Mr."
in front of their names.

Powerless, we punched
price keys with a vengeance,
slammed merchandise
across abrasive counters,
wondered what would happen
if the tables were turned.

SCENE OF THE CRIME

Boyfriends

I consider them emotional herpes,
past loves that bankrupted trust,
caused irreversible damage.
Ex-boyfriends and husbands
I am still trying to remove
from checking and credit card accounts.
They linger in houses once mine,
enjoy furniture and possessions
left behind, hold my clothes
and books hostage.
Their surprise communications
tear off the scabs,
destroy equilibrium,
cause painful flare-ups.
I don't want to reconnect,
stay in touch with their mothers,
meet new wives and offspring,
return old photos or albums,
forgive and forget,
let bygones be bygones.

Nothing to Declare

Jack travels light:
no suitcase, computer,
cell phone, companion.
Works temporary jobs,
just long enough
to finance airfare
for exotic adventures.
Has lived in an Oregon commune,
Israeli kibbutz, Korean village.
Slept with Bangkok transsexuals,
Amsterdam whores, knocked up
a New York underwear model.
Paid for the abortion.
Pushing sixty, he crashes
with friends, has no pension,
family obligations,
fixed address.
Leaves no loose ends,
human wreckage,
or carbon footprint
behind him.

Pike Place Public Market

I have wandered into alien territory.
An albino transvestite asks if I know
the world as we know it has ended.
He is framed by two homeless women
swaddled beside ragged dogs
within filthy blankets.
A toothless musician sits upon
a plastic bucket, rattles Starbucks cups
filled with percussive pebbles.
"I am soooo fucked up,"
the chick falling out of a
passing pedicab announces.
Fish mongers hawk slabs of halibut,
pink salmon cadavers.
The hulking black guy dressed
as a turquoise tyrannosaurus
twists red and green balloons
into improbable animals.
I cross the intersection,
am accosted by an activist
clutching a clipboard.
He rants about the injustices
wreaked by a corrupt legal system.
The bike cop arrives on cue,
clears a swath to permit passage
of cash-wielding tourists.

Tenacity

Until recently, she charged
through life like an Italian
Energizer Bunny.
Now she can't bend over,
plant flowers, pull weeds,
power walk.

"Don't tell me I'm doing
as well as can be expected
for a woman my age!"

Mom, 86, furious
because her doctor
can find no reason for
her shortness of breath.

"Slow down," I tell her.
She ignores me.
Tells me this is no time
to take it easy.
"I've got places to go,
people to see.
Goddammit to hell,
I am not getting old."

Chance Encounter

He's a grizzled dude
dressed in black
with long, curly hair.
Our paths cross daily,
him walking a geriatric
Labrador retriever.
As I hand Molly
her dog treat,
he starts conversation.
"You manage to solve
all the world's problems
over coffee this morning?"
Usually, it's a hat tip.
 "Mornin' ladies!" drawled
 as my sister and I pass
on our way to the post office.
Today he pauses, turns around,
goes our direction.
Asks if we like old rock and rollers.
Tells us he played bass guitar
in a band for Elvis Presley.
Tried starting his own group,
but doesn't get along
well with others.
He's heading south
to Big Sur and Nepenthe.
I recommend an Ambrosia Burger,
describe my center-stage birthdays,
full goddess drag, tiaras and blinis.
"I bet you and your friends light up
the deck, know how to party."
He's meeting folks
to celebrate the wrap
of his new solo album.
"See you gals tomorrow,"
he grins. "O.K. if I bring you CDs,
personally autographed copies?"

Trapped

For eighty years
Dad could haul himself
up and down sheer Sierra canyons
with a fishing creel and pole,
find deep pools, cast a line,
hook rainbow trout.
Now, after a botched surgery
and damaged spinal cord,
my father is immobile, diagnosed
with congestive heart failure,
put on an oxygen machine,
13 medications,
confined to the house.
Mom has confiscated his truck keys
so he can't escape to the orchard
with his Ford Explorer and dog.
Swim sessions at the YMCA
are a thing of the past.
Dad is an outdoor man,
needs dirt beneath his boots,
a rifle in his hands,
feels trapped and depressed.
Every indoor hour lasts for centuries.
His connections with
a world now denied
are TV, a cell phone.
Through windows he watches
life grow smaller,
the walls claustrophobic.
Numbered days drag.

Booth Bunny

Mac World, New York City, 1997

I share the Roseland lobby
with a bearded transsexual
pedaling an over-sized tricycle.
We greet guests attending
the software firm's gala.
S/he rides in a circle,
wears glitter, feathered angel wings,
a ballerina's white tutu.

I dispense drink tickets,
vouchers for palm readings,
mock tattoos, photo ops
with the band.
Instructed to circulate,
I hand out boxer shorts
emblazoned with the company's logo,
a *Size Does Matter* slogan.

I'm 47, have two master's degrees,
on my fifth shot
and last nerve,
can't believe how far
I've fallen.

Night School

He's six foot five,
dressed in torn Levi's,
flip-flops, faded
Grateful Dead tee shirt,
reeks of marijuana,
arrives in the computer lab
thirty minutes after
class has started.

"I have a few issues,"
he tells me,
hands over forms
requesting accommodation,
shares the names and numbers
of his probation officer
and court-appointed psychiatrist.

The following week,
Leonard is at his workstation,
barefoot and shirtless.
Agitated, he explains how
the FBI has stolen his files,
homework to be
turned in this evening.

Red-eyed and shaking,
he hands me a scuffed,
dirt-caked, cracked floppy disk.
The blue eagle, talons extended,
tattooed across his naked chest,
pulls my eyes from the crosses
carved onto each knuckle.

Grabbing my wrist, Leonard pleads,
explains how federal agents
are trying their best
to frame and destroy him.

It's going to be
eighteen difficult weeks till
this semester is over.

Santa Cruz

A barefoot freak parade meanders
from beachfront to Capitola
where it is perpetually 1970.
Hippie girls, braless under tie-dyed tee shirts,
emerge from psychedelic VW busses,
crowd the boardwalk, ankle bells tinkling,
exuding patchouli.

Reggae music and the smell of dope
permeate every corner.
Blonde surfer boys suck down ganja,
wax their boards, impress tattooed groupies.
I see myself stepping from the past,
a skinny chick in flip-flops, dangling earrings,
ass-length hair, signature tank top.

Former Students for a Democratic Society
hang with LSD pioneers at the Saturn Café.
We sip chai or herbal tea, a graying
collection of once-radical dropouts
washed ashore from the turbulent '60s.
We've replaced acid and hash with
Prilosec, Celebrex, Prozac,
don't share mattresses or tantric sex
with each other's lovers.

These days, we gather and bitch
like every generation before us,
describe the enlightened utopia
of health, happiness and harmony
we could create and inhabit
if we weren't on fixed incomes
and so damned exhausted.

Public Library Service

Some think my job is great,
imagine I read all day.
Till I tell them
of drunk, homeless
psychotics, the stoned
and enraged ones
seeking refuge at tables,
hiding overnight
in library bathrooms.
Guessing which
delusional outpatient might
stab, shoot or stalk me.
How do I describe
latchkey kids,
abandoned here by
crack-whore mothers?
Pimps and pushers
who drop by afternoons,
check out future
junkies and hookers.
Pregnant ten-year-olds
raped by older brothers,
stepfathers, uncles.
What it feels like
unlocking burglar bars
at 9 a.m. every morning,
offering throwaway children
sanctuary for a few hours.

P.S.

Despite the restraining order,
he sends you an email,
tells you he misses
the free morning paper,
someone paying bills,
cooking special meals,
giving him blow jobs.
He says it's too bad
it's cost your mother
$60,000 this year
for your rent, gasoline,
buying your groceries.
He is living with four guys
in a friend's spacious mansion,
wishes you hadn't screwed
up his last body-building contest
by having him served, then arrested.
No apologies or restitution
for the money he owes you.
At the end, he expresses
his misery at the way
things are now, for him.
By the way, he still loves you.

Lost

Street names or direction
didn't matter to Mom.
Each trip was an adventure.
She ignored dead ends,
speed limits, empty gas tanks,
fixated on destination,
failed to note her surroundings,
was amnesiac when it came
to geographic landmarks
or roadside details.
I spent a stressed childhood
witnessing frantic toll calls
for better directions
which she sought, then ignored.

Once at a restaurant,
she used the restroom
while Dad and I returned
to wait in the car.
Fifteen minutes later,
my cell phone rang.
She was in a panic,
had used a different exit,
couldn't find the correct parking lot,
thought we'd left her behind.
"Anytime I want to get rid of your mother,"
my father once drawled,
"I'd just spin her around
for three revolutions
and let her go.
She'd wander for eternity,
never find me again."
The thought made him smile.

Life in the Early Bracero

We were volatile and vocal,
musicians, poets, photographers,
sharing a flophouse
on the wrong side of the tracks
in the barrio section of town.
Here the door was always open,
cold beer plentiful, more than enough
wine and weed to go around.
Parties were spontaneous and continual.
Once started, the feasting and fighting
could extend for weeks at a time.
Anyone might be scribbling poetry
at the kitchen table,
loading blues onto the stereo turntable,
filming an experimental video,
committing adultery,
playing exquisite corpse,
performing passionate art.
Strangers would wander in to verify rumors,
take one look and run like hell.
We were a family of washed-ashore misfits,
emotionally damaged, economically unstable,
the most creative we would be
for the rest of our lives.

I Got My Guns at Al's

Made famous by Elmore Leonard,
it's the gym
where professional boxers trained;
parolees and welter weights
hefted, grimaced and groaned.

They sneered at my puny poundage,
a flat-chested, pissed-off divorcee,
the only woman in sight, silently
slamming 200 pounds straight up,
with muscular legs.

I watched them watching me,
homies I recognized
from the county honor farm
and my bookmobile route,
muscle-bound Aryans
who talked tough from
behind a curling iron,
sold real estate or insurance by days.

They showed me photos
of women bodybuilders,
wondered if I was a dyke
but never asked.

We all had reasons, routines
and a common goal:
invulnerability.

On the Town

The barrista at Fermentations
shows me the sixteen stitches
over her eyebrow, tells me
how the local physician's assistant
sewed her up for only $35.
She promises an introduction,
my insurance against
future tanked-up disasters,
says when I move here,
we'll be best buds forever.

At Mozzi's, old drunken hippies
play rotation pool.
Nailed to the ceiling,
a wagon wheel light, signs
from bankrupt local businesses.
Over-the-hill sluts shriek,
expose more side boob
than necessary,
take up all the bar stools.

A bright yellow poster
hangs on the door:
Guys: No Shirt–No Service
Gals: No Shirt–Free Drinks
This is my kingdom;
these are my people.

Marginalized and Mad

People detour around Susan
rummaging through the garbage cans
on Ocean Avenue in Carmel.
She sees their eyes as mirrors,
her reflection a frightening demon,
and hears a clutter of voices in her head.

Every day we meet on the sidewalk near Doud Arcade.
When she looks up, I smile, wish her a good morning.
She mumbles hello, remembers my name,
then slides back into a private world
while cursing, throwing trash and empty cans.
The visitors who don't know her
cross to the other side of the street.

Sometimes I wonder what chemical imbalance
could push me off the same ledge where
Susan and I would forage among discards
and together shriek in frustration, furious
at the cosmos or whatever got in our way.

Coffee Klatch

Something compels me
to visit the donut & coffee shop
where my dead father
and his cronies
used to hang out.
Farmers, ag supply salesmen
occupy every table, drink in
right-wing political commentary,
local gossip, sexist remarks.
Not another woman in sight.
To even the odds,
I invite a female cousin
to join my sister and myself
for a cup of terrible brew.
We commandeer space,
force men to move from chairs
they've always called theirs.
We shriek, compare men's laughter
to the sound of untuned Harleys,
share priceless phrases
we've just overheard.
Unable to adjust
to women with opinions,
geezers grumble;
we've invaded
good-old-boy territory.
Twenty minutes later,
we've run off the last of them,
declare the place ours,
a testosterone-free zone,
plan our next offensive,
tip the counter girl well.

Punitive Loss

Orders came for
a Cape Flattery
lifeboat station.
We had 48 hours
to make arrangements,
then move.
Traded my Mustang
for a station wagon and cash.
Put down money
on a small mobile home.
My husband was 21,
just home from 'Nam.
I was 19, pregnant, stressed.
That night contractions began.
By morning, our baby was gone.
We loaded what little
we had left, followed
semi and trailer house
onto the ferry.
Drove for hours
on a dirt road
to the Makah Reservation.
Three years of isolated duty
as punishment for my
anti-war protest.
He was military; I was civilian.
We both served the sentence.

Domestic Violence

He pulls doorknobs from shattered wood,
crushes wicker chairs,
cracks the glass kitchen table,
raises bruises and welts.

When he commands, your fingers
prepare his steroid syringes,
plunge a needle past hard muscle,
ding solid bone.

"Cancer is the disease of resentment," you said.
During the months of chemotherapy,
he piled pillows against your writhing body,
left you seizing in a closet by yourself.

Now, you pack and evict his wreckage,
trade news clippings and Ironman trophies
to reclaim and resurrect
your old unbroken self.

Dr. Nazi's Poetry Workshop

You know the type:
white, middle-aged, male.
Flaunts his MFA.
Hasn't been laid
by a woman with a brain
for at least twenty years.
Runs his workshop
like a poetry pogrom.
Complains your work is
too realistic, hard-edged.
Lavishes attention
on the rhyming blonde
with enormous breasts.
Knocks back beers
alongside a slam poet
wearing tight leather pants.
His red pencil
tortures your lines,
removes the teeth
from a story.
Turns your voice into
an imitation of his.
Suggests asphyxiation
by adjectives
as a final solution.

Succubus Soulmates

We exchange unhappiness,
piss and moan,
complain about partners.
Do nothing
to extricate ourselves
from bad/sad situations.
Make excuses to avoid
rocking the boat:
Finances. Fear.
Family obligations.
Change requires risk,
mustering courage.
We cling to the familiar,
limp along, tolerate
sharp stones
we could remove
from shoes
to ease the pain
but don't.
Embrace accustomed roles
as martyr and cripple.

Scene of the Crime

"My life has a superb cast but I can't figure out the plot."
—Ashleigh Brilliant

45 years, three husbands later,
I board a plane, return to Seattle.
This time, the hotel is upscale,
no convention of Shriners
running up and down hallways.
I'm not navigating steep
slippery cobblestone streets
in a Ford Mustang during a rainstorm.
No U-Haul filled with my earthly possessions
chained to a parking garage pillar.

I am older, not wiser,
here to make peace with the past,
explore better options.
My perspective has altered.
The Space Needle that once terrified
seems diminutive compared to
modern skyscrapers that now surround it.
I'll revisit the scene of old crimes,
remember that 19-year-old child bride,
first time away from home,
married less than 48 hours,
realizing her fatal mistake,
crying her eyes out.

SOBERANES FIRE

Ignition: Day 1

Conflagration consumes forest,
ignites structures, chaparral,
explodes ridgetops, spews ashy plumes.

Firefighters doze protective barriers,
clear-cut trees, back-burn vegetation,
attempt to corral omniverous flames.

Smoky murk infiltrates canyons,
smothers nearby villages,
exudes unbreathable reek.

Hell's insatiable perimeter expands.
Soot identifies blasted hillsides.
Seething wildfire blooms.

Pall: Day 2, 0% Containment

Cinders combine with compromised fog.
Yellowish murk oozes north and south.
Sick reek nullifies sunrise.
Ash sprinkles from flaming juggernaut,
exploding gray plumes.

Smoke drapes its diseased pall
over charred hillsides,
cremated forest,
spills sooty ruin
into watersheds, ocean.

We tremble on the abyss
of mandatory evacuation.
Relentless combustion
consumes pines, cypress,
oaks, outbuildings, homes.

Friends gather irreplaceable
documents, artwork, medications.
Load family, pets into vehicles,
prepare to flee just ahead of
the fiery storm.

Triage: Day 3, 5% Containment

As conflagration advances,
what do you save?
Family, photos, artwork?
Prescriptions, pets?
Ravenous fire erases landmarks,
memories both good and bad.

Your eyes stream while ripping away
roses, geraniums, shrubs,
ornamental grasses, trees close to the house;
sacrifice what you once nurtured,
apply flame-retardant foam,
blame tears on acrid smoke.

Reckoning: Day 10, 18% Containment

Fifty-seven family homes incinerated,
42,000 acres, including parkland, consumed.
Firefighters stream to base camps from
myriad West Coast communities.
Today, air tankers and helicopters are grounded,
blinded by a combination of thick fog and smoke.

Ground crews dig protective boundaries,
ignite back-burns, hope the dozer lines hold.
Fine ash falls, coats every surface.
Morning walks along Carmel Beach
now require an emergency inhaler,
protective eye coverings, surgical mask.

Reek: Day 13, 25% containment

Ashy reek erases hillsides and sun.
Air quality degenerates.
Employees in Big Sur
and Carmel Valley
are warned to leave,
work somewhere else.

In Marina, dogs sniff smoky atmosphere,
refuse to go out.
Clothes, carpets, drapes smell
like the smoldering campfire
that started this blaze.
Shrubs and outdoor tables disappear
beneath a constant bombardment
of powdery dust.

Cause & Consequence: Day 14, 27% Containment

In between community meetings, the command chief
schedules a televised press conference,
says he has an announcement.

Grim men stand beside him as he reveals
the results of days-long investigation:
conflagration caused by unattended, illegal campfire.

Last night's satellite sweep reveals active expansion
along Launtz Ridge as wildfire burns its way
toward Ventana Double Cone, Big Sur River watershed.

Hot imagery appears near Little Pines and Uncle Sam Mountain.
Today's statistics: 51,000 acres destroyed,
one death, homes and memories reduced to ash.

Concours d'Conflagration: Day 15, 35% containment

Overnight, another five thousand acres vanish,
vaporized by voracious fire's roiling run.
Dani Ridge, Jackson Camp and Post Summit are tinder,
will soon blaze into charred oblivion.

Crews doze, back-burn East Molera Ridge,
protect campgrounds, cabins, cliffside resorts
while incoming caravans of Bentleys, Rolls Royces,
Ferraris, Maseratis, clog all the roads.

Carmel Valley and Big Sur smolder as
the Concours d'Elegance, an annual car show
for arrogant millionaires and their groupies,
carelessly rolls into town.

The Remains: Day 16, 40% Containment

Evacuees first learn of their losses
when video of charred houses, scorched bikes,
melted appliances appear on local TV.

Those choosing to shelter in place were required
to provide authorities copies of dental records.
The displaced chafe to return, view smoking remains.

The lucky ones allowed back in tell of seared land,
propane tanks transformed into fire bombs,
a few lucky homes spared.

Some are antsy for insurance adjusters
to record devastation, photograph rubble,
get to work on filing their claims.

Others debate whether they have the will
to assess damage, inventory losses,
rebuild upon sooty ruins.

Evacuation of Big Sur: Day 17, 45% Containment

A reverse 911 call comes at 3:11 a.m.
Fire has jumped the southern containment line.
Flames ignite ridges east of Mt. Manual,
revisit terrain devastated in 2008 by the
Basin Complex/Ventana Wilderness burn.
Consumed acreage swells.

The Monterey County Sheriff's Office orders
a mandatory evacuation for the Big Sur Area
from Point Sur Lighthouse to Deetjen's Inn,
Henry Miller Memorial Library and Nepenthe
in its fiery path, both sides of Highway 1.

Tourists are allowed free access
to evacuated areas while residents
are ordered to pack necessities, hit the road north.
In Carmel Valley, air tankers and helicopters
load supplies, hotshot crews, and finally take flight.

Displaced: Day 18, 45% Containment

60,000+ acres have now been consumed.
Fire retardant bleeds against
scorched hills, denuded canyons,
blackened pine ruins.
Seared oaks, sooty manzanita,
protrude like burnt bones
from scarred, smoking land.

The upside: total annihilation of poison oak.
On the downside: dispossessed bobcats,
hungry deer, tense mountain lions wander
into populated villages, driven out
by fiery, falling trees, cremated terrain.

Squirrels and cottontails perish.
Hawks, blackbirds and condors disappear.
Trapped field mice succumb,
incinerated by100-foot walls
of roiling flame.

Smolder: Day 19, 50% Containment

By now, over 67,000 acres have burned.
Smoke wreathes coastal ranges.
Fire runs into Big Sur Valley.
Satellite sweeps reveal the heat perimeter
expanding south and east.

Rumors and second-guessing abound.
Were air tankers erroneously stopped
from scooping ocean water because of
the sanctuary status of Monterey Bay?
What if cell phone coverage had been available,
permitting faster reporting, response?
Why didn't crew commanders enlist assistance
from locals familiar with rugged terrain?

Hand-lettered signs, commercial banners
thanking firefighters line street shoulders.
One friend cynically posts on social media,
"How could one little campfire possibly hurt?"

Costs: Day 20, 50% Containment

We wake to another morning of reek.
Smoke from blazing Ventana Wilderness
drifts north and east upon ocean winds.
Falling ash from combusted forests
coats shrubs, clings to cars.
It's been three weeks of angst,
evacuation, road closures, ruin.

The cost of fighting fire
runs over $6 million per day.
Big Sur businesses forced to close.
Death, injuries, PTSD.
70,000 incinerated acres.
Homes and other structures
damaged, destroyed.

Expensive air tankers, helicopters
lift off when visibility permits,
dump water scooped from the ocean
onto accessible hot spots,
spread pricey red retardant
against flaming hills.

We wait for Armageddon
to burn itself out.

Smoke: Day 21, 55% Containment

Air quality plummets as prevailing winds
push stench and ash north.
Outdoor breathing is hazardous.
Those with lung conditions
or sensitivities are warned
to stay inside, keep windows closed.

Further south, crews back-fire brush
to clear room for firefighting equipment
at Andrew Molera State Park.
Reek from multiple hot spots
drifts above Lone Pine Camp,
Ventana Double Cone,
strangles Carmel, Monterey,
Seaside, Marina.

Watsonville, Aromas, Santa Cruz
are now affected, smothered by smoke.
It's unsafe to hike, bike, visit beaches.
Every breath singes the lungs.

Firing North Coast Ridge Road: Day 23, 60% Containment

Hotshots with drip torches ignite underbrush,
work their way along rugged dirt road.
Crews labor twenty-four hour shifts, inhale ashy smoke,
back-burn from containment line, deny advancing blaze
vulnerable homes, chaparral, any flammable fuel.
They focus, not on orange flames, but on green,
look for flyaway sparks.
We give thanks for morning's drippy fog,
Ventana Double Cone's granite face.

Officials move the staging camp from Carmel Valley
to California State University, Monterey Bay,
nearly an hour north of where needed,
repurpose golf course to accommodate carriers
for upcoming Car Week's expensive designer vehicles.
Therapists offer free PTSD counseling.
Local poets and musicians raise funds
to assist the displaced.

Combustion vs. Carmageddon: Day 26, 60% Containment

Highway 1 South reopens as CalFire continues
removing blasted redwoods, burnt vegetation.
Portions of roadway have buckled from heat.
The power company replaces destroyed poles, melted wire.
In Cachagua, crews begin restoration, evaluate charred terrain.

Twenty-six miles north, Carmel barricades side streets
and main thoroughfare to permit an all-day display
of vintage Porches and Ferraris.
Monterey erects a tent over Custom House Plaza,
Sotheby's auction site, to prevent falling ash from
marring the paint of rare luxury cars.

Picking Up the Pieces: Day 27, 60% Containment

As residents return to smoke-saturated homes,
start rebuilding, repairing damage,
car enthusiasts continue to pour into town,
fill hotels, overflow highways,
carelessly abuse locals and landscape
with self-entitled behaviors.

When the winds shift,
smoke drifts above sand and ocean,
wends between cottages,
over tinder-dry urban forest.
To date, 76,000 acres devoured.

High-end rental chateaus sport Bentleys,
Aston Martins, Maseratis, Ferraris.
A luxury yacht, anchored
just off Pebble Beach,
floats within sight of a celebrity golf course.
The 1% clutter Carmel's exclusive bistros,
ignore stop signs, bike lanes, pedestrians,
assault a traumatized community.

While Rome Burns: Day 28, 60% Containment

Overnight, conflagration makes a run
along Mt. Olmstead into Cold Springs.
By morning, 80,000 acres have burned.
Estimated containment date is revised
to the end of October, dependent on rain.

Wind gusts and low humidity fuel
the most fire activity in over a week,
push flames to Lion Creek.
Blaze approaches Carmel River.
Tassajara Zen Center is tense but prepared,
fire only ten miles away.

Porches, Lamborghinis, Ferraris
drag race Highway 1 from Cambria
to Carmel, ignore ongoing devastation,
illegally pass on sheer cliffside curves.

Priorities: Day 29, 60% Containment

No Parking signs along Carmel Valley Road
ensuring rapid first responder access are disregarded.
More disappear from the roadside near Rancho Canada.
As week five unfolds, 81,000 acres have burned.
Cost of containment now totals around $174,000,000.

In Monterey, white tents are erected to facilitate
the weekend's rare auto auctions.
Sotheby's estimates sales will yield
in excess of $100,000,000;
a 1962 Shelby 260 Cobra is expected
to sell for over $20,000,000.

Just north of Custom House Plaza,
volunteers serve hot breakfast
for a ragged assemblage of the homeless.
Fire crosses Carmel River near Hiding Camp.
To the south, Partington Ridge smolders.

Gratitude: Day 30, 60% Containment

Swollen moon, tinted orange by hovering smoke,
soars above charred hills, blackened trees,
spared Zen monastery, saved family homes.
Pale light showers evacuees, ruins.

As conflagration enters week five,
signs thanking firefighters burgeon.
Work crews erase bulldozer scars, restore
damaged parkland, rebuild wilderness trails.

At an organic farm stand, donors mingle,
sip Carmel Valley wine,
nibble chicken curry, fruit and cheese.
Local authors read prose and verse.

Humor lightens hearts. Poetry heals.
Overhead, chattering helicopters
carry water to dump on fresh hot spots,
extinguish spark-scattering flares.

Flare Up: Day 70, 81% Containment

Despite low humidity, rising winds,
the ten-week-old fire
moves toward total containment.

Slop-over that threatened Tassajara
is corralled by back-burns, aerial drops
of pond water, scarlet retardant.

A rogue flare up near blackened Mt. Manuel
causes momentary worry, but satellite imaging
reveals no new Carmel River watershed hot spots.

Locals wonder if it will ever end.
128,000+ acres have burned.
Bad air besmirches every horizon.

Apocalypse Aftermath: Day 83, 100% Containment

Predicted rains will drown
the remains of smoldering fire—
enough to squelch flames but
not trigger debris flows.

Slowly, wildlife returns
to blackened hillsides,
sooty canyons,
ash-covered valley.

Already, weeds reappear.
Gray meadows reveal tender green.
Tiny redwoods and pines sprout
from fog-dampened cinders.

MALPRACTICE

Malpractice

For six months
Mom has complained
of stomach pain
to her impatient doctor.
His records document
breast cancer surgery,
chemotherapy, radiation,
spread of malignant cells
into her stomach.

Despite her history,
no new scans are ordered.
He tells her she's
just getting old.
The breathlessness,
exhaustion and weight loss,
common symptoms of aging.

When she develops bloating,
severe constipation,
he prescribes an
over-the-counter laxative,
sends her off for an X-ray,
says all is normal.

A week after she collapses
from debilitating diarrhea,
is taken to Emergency by paramedics,
a consulting gastroenterologist
discovers an intestinal blockage.
Seven days later, a surgeon
opens her to reveal
the inoperable cancer.

Turfed

There is zero privacy
once you are admitted,
confined to a hospital bed.
You shed clothes, dignity,
give yourself over
to uncommunicative doctors,
unfathomable procedures.
People with unreadable name tags
wander in and out, checking blood pressure,
temperature, pulse.
Every act is public.
Beeps, needle sticks interrupt rest.
It is impossible to sleep
undisturbed through the night.
Others make life-and-death
decisions on your behalf.
You are one more medical mystery,
dysfunctional organ, chronic condition,
extensively tested, prodded and probed.
The length of your confinement
is indeterminate.
Hours elongate, melt together.
You lose all landmarks.
The sterile walls have no clocks.

Like a B Movie

An interchangeable cast
of cranky actors costumed as nurses
or white-coated specialists
move in and out
of your hospital room.

They ignore the name
listed above your bed,
printed upon wristband,
wordlessly perform a variety
of medical functions.

So far, they've pricked
your finger, mistaking you
for the unresponsive diabetic
on the opposite gurney.

Administered respiratory therapy
intended for a guy across the hall.
Tried to dose you with
the incorrect chemo.

Food Service bungles
90% of your orders.
Twice they forget
to deliver your dinner.

Over and over
you remind them
you can walk on your own
when they insist
on a walker or wheelchair.

You wonder if the pathology report
of metastasized malignancy
actually belongs to you.
Try to convince yourself
it's just one more mistake.

After the Verdict

Mom has been on the table
only an hour and a half when
the surgeon and her assistant
pull us out of the waiting room.
Both are in tears.
Cancer everywhere, inoperable.
They will close her up,
send her back to her room.
Work out a plan to keep
her pain-free.

She takes the news stoically.
Says she knew already,
expected the worse.
Tells me to be sure the
health insurance company
issues a refund.
Dictates a simple funeral,
no more than 90 minutes
for a public viewing.

Her final demand:
Forget saying the rosary.
"Make sure they don't
make me up like
a damned Kewpie doll."

Comfortably Numb

The trick is medicating ahead
of inevitable pain.
I endure excruciating days
beside Mom's bed, bolstered
by caffeine and carbohydrates
followed by Valium.
She is tethered to saline
and slow Tylenol drip.

We know it will never get better.
Complain about politics, Donald Trump.
Talk around the subject of death.
Sleep when possible.
Eat what we can swallow.
Find new ways to adapt.
I am there to bear witness,
organize caregivers,
provide comfort.

The surgeon explains how
they will place dissolvable tabs
under her tongue.
When the time comes,
let her slip away peacefully.
For those that love her,
there will be no escape.

Hospice

We acknowledge
the absence of hope
by signing a contract.
Agree to conditions:
no calling 911,
attempting radiation,
chemotherapy or resuscitation.

Today they deliver
hospital bed,
walker, commode.
A pharmacy delivers
an assorted collection
of terminal drugs.

They advise family
about administering
morphine tablets,
liquid methadone,
fever suppositories.
Warn it won't be long
before she is unresponsive,
taken to a peaceful place
beyond tortuous pain.

Life Expectancy

My aunt with dementia
calls the process of death
Mom's "ongoing project."
Daily, her energy levels vary.
Depression comes and goes.
She enjoys visitors but,
if they stay too long,
they leave her exhausted.

She tells me which bills to pay,
how to handle taxes, paperwork,
record expenditures, income.
Asks me to hide valuables
in my other aunt's house.
Fears healthcare workers
might take bankbooks,
steal her jewelry.

Last night her own mother
appeared in a dream,
promised it would all be okay.
Today she describes what outfit
and accessories to she wants used
when consigned to her coffin.

She asks how long she will live,
if she will suffer.
The hospice doctor says
it's between her and God.

Home Sweet Home

Hospice arranges transport,
delivers the necessary equipment
because Mom wants to come home.
Gentle paramedics maneuver
her gurney across threshold,
navigate narrow hallway,
settle her into the hospital bed
in the den where she will spend
the rest of her life.

She is able to breakfast
at the kitchen table,
shuffle two or three laps
around the living room
with her walker before
snuggling into leather recliner
with paper, blanket,
steaming hot toddy.

Friends and neighbors
arrive in shifts
to deliver flowers,
pay their final respects.
Soon every surface
is covered with bouquets,
chilling precursor
of inevitable funeral day.

Doing or Dying

Mom, 89 years old,
wasn't aware
God was listening
when she said she
didn't want to turn 90.

Weeks later,
she was hospitalized,
diagnosed with terminal,
inoperable cancer.

Now she's home,
enrolled in hospice,
unable to eat food she loves.
Can't bake, garden or move
without walker
or caregiver assistance.

Tires easily.
Gets confused.
Fears coming pain.
Hopes it's over
before the holidays come.

Wishes she could
peacefully go to sleep
and never wake up—
just like my Dad.

Says this is no way to live.
She's Catholic, however,
wants death with dignity
but cannot let go.

Dietician

Mom's hospice dietician
enumerates the limited palette
of what she can eat.
What foods to avoid.
What will bind or inflame.

For nearly two months,
she has survived on vegetable broth,
popsicles, jello,
bland cream of rice.
Has lost over twenty-five pounds,
eyes sunken, skin drawn,
growing weaker by day.

Tells me if this is her life
from now until death,
she'd rather refuse nourishment,
just go to sleep, get it over with,
never wake up again.

Autumn Harvest

On the almond trees,
fuzzy green nuts swell,
split their skins,
dry to brittle maturity
in hot summer sun.

Mom shrinks from
lack of nourishment,
eyes sunken,
bones protruding.
She is wasting away.

It's September,
time for harvest,
life to let go,
transition,
be gathered in.

Sustenance

Mom is tired of soft,
clear or bland.
Craves scampi,
fettucine Alfredo,
a huge juicy cheeseburger.
She suffers an inoperable
intestinal blockage,
will never eat solids again.

"What's the point of living?"
she complains as we tempt her
with mashed banana,
scrambled egg whites,
exotic cream soups
which she rejects as too salty,
too tasteless, too sweet.

Popsicles and orange sherbet
are her remaining luxuries,
cruel irony for a woman
who baked rich wine cake,
luscious chocolate pies,
persimmon cookies,
fragrant biscotti.

Afterlife

Mom's niece and nephew
visit once the family grapevine
has spread news
of her terminal cancer.

When company arrives,
she dresses up,
holds court from
her living room sofa.

My cousin had been worried, dialed
Mom's cell phone time after time
but got no response,
battery dead.

Mom wonders about the afterlife,
if she'll be reunited with
pre-deceased husband,
daughter, granddaughter.

Relatives ask her to let them know
from the other side, once she finds out.
"I'll call you on my cell," she promises.
Makes everyone laugh.

The Visitors

Once Mom is home,
they arrive in shifts—
friends, family,
hospice workers and nurse.

Some recognize when she tires,
make graceful excuses and go.
Others overstay their welcome,
leave her drawn and wiped out.

After the first week,
traffic diminishes.
No new cards or flowers,
fewer visitors appear.

Ebbing mortality
slowly expires.
In shadowy corners,
Death bides its time.

Autumn Deadheading

Mom frets over losing control.
Other people make decisions
that shape what's left of her life.
She is comforted by creating lists,
questioning caregivers,
issuing orders.

I follow her detailed instructions,
strip willow seedlings
from planting beds
beneath low-hanging foliage,
stuff weeded spurge and oxalis
into white plastic bucket.

It's autumn, the time of year
to cut back spent petunias,
rake fallen leaves,
snap off dead hydrangea blooms,
prune plum trees and roses.

I plant yellow pansies,
dwarf snapdragons,
harbingers of spring.
We pretend she'll be around
to enjoy their bright flowers.

Methadone Blues

My sister weeps
seeing our mother curled up
in her hospital bed
looking like a starved baby bird
that has fallen out of its nest.

Mom wears her silly pink sweater
with a goofy dog printed on the front,
baggy black sweat pants,
favorite blue robe,
warm fuzzy socks.

Earlier, she tried sitting up,
moved from plastic-wrapped mattress
to her comfy recliner,
attempted to visit
but kept nodding off.

Methadone erases pain,
causes vertigo,
transforms her from
opinionated authoritarian
into a confused, querulous child.

Even the lowest dosage
upsets her stomach,
brings hallucinations, tears,
a wish to die quickly while unconscious.
She sleeps eighteen hours a day.

Grace

Unsettled skies part,
spill celestial rays,
illuminate shabby barn,
dust-shrouded orchard.

Brief illusion bestows grace—
upon mortal confusions:
approaching death, confused grief,
jarring passage of seasons.

From her hospital bed,
Mom feels life ebbing away,
admires blushing peach tree,
autumn's red and gold foliage.

Restoration

Depleted spirits recharge
during an afternoon walk
among white sage,
pliant willows,
along lazy kinks of river.

I explore sand bars, silted snags,
remember fishing here with my father.
During autumn, battered salmon swam upstream,
gills heaving when lifted off hooks,
their journey to old spawning grounds interrupted.

Dad is gone; Mom, terminally ill, will soon join him.
I return to childhood's compromised sanctuary,
assaulted by grief and anger,
wash away emotional pain
soothed by restorative water.

Crepe Myrtle

for my mother, 6/5/27–7/20/17

Hot pink blooms dance
in delta breeze, spill confetti
among glossy foliage,
vivid metaphors that mimic
the jaunty scarlet jacket
mom wears within
polished oak casket.

Stubborn shrubs thrive
on soaring temperatures,
bounce back from hard winter frosts.
Mom defied her terminal prognosis,
obstinately endured for months,
refused to relinquish normal daily routines:
getting dressed to meet company,
putting on makeup.

Today we bury her
among husband, mother,
daughter, granddaughter.
In the garden, Blue Lily of the Nile
surround flowering tree,
salute her ascending soul,
serve as regal reminders.

Acknowledgments

Blue Monday Review: "Public Library Service"

Brickplight: "Scene of the Crime"

The Creativity Web Site: "Turfed"

Dead Snakes: "Booth Bunny," "Punitive Loss," "On the Town," "Home Sweet Home"

The Five-Two Crime Poetry Blog: "Dr. Nazi's Poetry Workshop," "Reek"

Foliate Oak Literary Magazine: "Santa Cruz"

I Am Not a Silent Poet: "Domestic Violence"

In Between Hangovers: "Nothing to Declare," "Pike Place Public Market," "I Got My Guns at Al's"

Nature Writing: "Restoration," "Crepe Myrtle"

Nerve Cowboy: "Life in the Early Bracero"

New Verse News: "Concours d'Conflagration," "Evacuation of Big Sur," "Smolder," "Firing North Coast Ridge Road," "Combustion vs. Carmageddon"

Plato's Tavern Open Mic: "Pall"

The Potomac: "Lost"

Red River Review: "Marginalized and Mad"

The Saturday Diner Open Mic: "Malpractice"

Silver Birch Press: "Namesake," "Guinevere," "In My *What the Hell* Hat," "Hard," "Are You Experienced?," "Doppelgänger," "Driver's Ed," "Autumn on Kauai," "Hanalei Halloween," "Cinderella's Support Group," "Exodus," "Gastronomical Archive," "Ho Ho Humbug," "If I Had Listened to Mom," "Mane Events," "Seduction," "Witch Hunt," "Sleuth," "Chain Store Hell"

Syndic Journal: "Coffee Klatch"

Unrorean: "P.S."

Wilderness House Literary Review: "Succubus Soulmates," "Boyfriends"

Your One Phone Call: "Like a B Movie"

Cover artwork by Gene McCormick; author photo by Laura Bayless; cover and interior book design by Diane Kistner; Chaparral Pro text and titling with Big Book

About FutureCycle Press

FutureCycle Press is dedicated to publishing lasting English-language poetry books, chapbooks, and anthologies in both print-on-demand and Kindle ebook formats. Founded in 2007 by long-time independent editor/publishers and partners Diane Kistner and Robert S. King, the press incorporated as a nonprofit in 2012. A number of our editors are distinguished poets and writers in their own right, and we have been actively involved in the small press movement going back to the early seventies.

The FutureCycle Poetry Book Prize and honorarium is awarded annually for the best full-length volume of poetry we publish in a calendar year. Introduced in 2013, our Good Works projects are anthologies devoted to issues of universal significance, with all proceeds donated to a related worthy cause. Our Selected Poems series highlights contemporary poets with a substantial body of work to their credit; with this series we strive to resurrect work that has had limited distribution and is now out of print.

We are dedicated to giving all of the authors we publish the care their work deserves, making our catalog of titles the most diverse and distinguished it can be, and paying forward any earnings to fund more great books.

We've learned a few things about independent publishing over the years. We've also evolved a unique, resilient publishing model that allows us to focus mainly on vetting and preserving for posterity poetry collections of exceptional quality without becoming overwhelmed with bookkeeping and mailing, fundraising activities, or taxing editorial and production "bubbles." To find out more about what we are doing, come see us at www.futurecycle.org.

The FutureCycle Poetry Book Prize

All full-length volumes of poetry published by FutureCycle Press in a given calendar year are considered for the annual FutureCycle Poetry Book Prize. This allows us to consider each submission on its own merits, outside of the context of a contest. Too, the judges see the finished book, which will have benefitted from the beautiful book design and strong editorial gloss we are famous for.

The book ranked the best in judging is announced as the prize-winner in the subsequent year. There is no fixed monetary award; instead, the winning poet receives an honorarium of 20% of the total net royalties from all poetry books and chapbooks the press sold online in the year the winning book was published. The winner is also accorded the honor of being on the panel of judges for the next year's competition; all judges receive copies of all contending books to keep for their personal library.

www.ingramcontent.com/pod-product-compliance
Lightning Source LLC
Chambersburg PA
CBHW070002100426
42741CB00012B/3104